CCSS **Genre** Expository Text

W9-AWQ-839

Essential Question
How do animals adapt to challenges in their habitat?

Life in a Tide Pool

by Mary Mackie

Chapter 1

A Changing World

Take a walk along a rocky beach and, if you look closely, you can see a whole world of creatures at your feet. There are clusters of mussels. Small snails cling to rocks. The green sea anemone waves its **tentacles** in the water. Crabs hide beneath rocks.

The world these animals live in is always changing. Twice a day, ocean water sweeps in and covers the land. Then the water rushes out again. Small pools of water are left behind, but the rest of the shore is dry.

Tide pool creatures live in a world that is always changing.

The small pools of water are called tide pools. Tide pools form in rocky areas where the land meets the sea. For example, one place you can find tide pools is along the rocky coast of California.

A tide pool is a **habitat** for many different plants and animals. A habitat is a place where a plant or an animal lives. It is a plant or animal's environment.

Crabs live in tide pools on rocky coasts.

The tide pool habitat is made up of areas called zones. These zones form between the lowest low tides and the highest high tides. The low tide zone is mostly underwater. It is only exposed when the tide is very low. The mid zone is exposed twice a day by the tides. The high tide zone is flooded at high tide. The splash zone is mostly dry but is splashed with salt water during high tides.

Tide pools change as the tide rises and falls.

High Tide and Low Tide

The tides are the regular rise and fall of the ocean. In most places, the tide rises and falls twice a day. At maximum height the rising tide is called high tide. When the falling tide reaches its lowest level it is called low tide.

Intertidal Zone Map

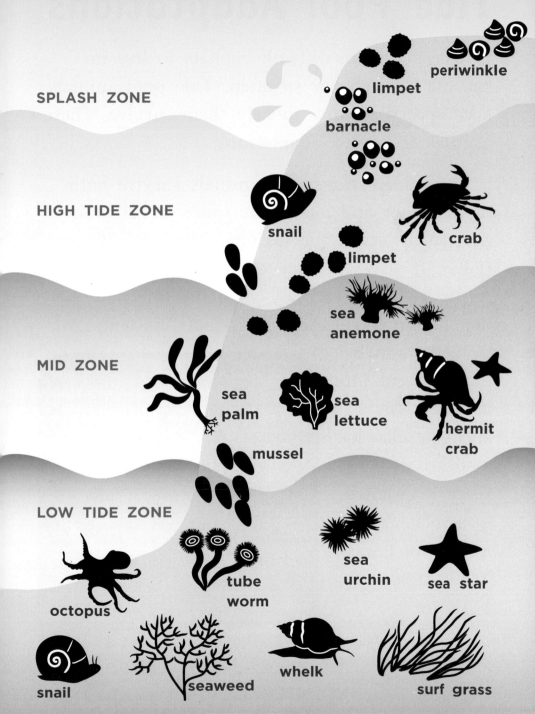

SPLASH ZONE

periwinkle

limpet

barnacle

HIGH TIDE ZONE

snail

crab

limpet

sea anemone

MID ZONE

sea palm

sea lettuce

hermit crab

mussel

LOW TIDE ZONE

octopus

tube worm

sea urchin

sea star

snail

seaweed

whelk

surf grass

Chapter 2

Tide Pool Adaptations

Tide pools are difficult habitats to live in because they change so often. Tide pool animals need special features to help them survive. These features are called **adaptations**.

Some adaptations help animals survive both in the water and out of the water. When it is covered by water, the sea anemone looks like a flower. It waves its long tentacles in the water, trying to catch fish. But when the tide pool is dry, the anemone changes. It hides its tentacles from the sun by pulling them into its body. The anemone also has a sucker disk that keeps it fastened to a rock. Strong waves won't wash it out to sea.

Sea anemones have sucker disks to hold on to rocks.

Barnacles, limpets, and mussels live in the splash zone. They are in the sun for much of the day. They have hard shells for protection. They are able to store water and food inside their shells. Snails, crabs, and hermit crabs also have shells for shelter and protection.

Barnacles, limpets, and mussels have adapted to life in the splash zone. They have hard shells that protect them from the sun.

Sea hares are hard to see among the rocks and plants in a tide pool.

Sometimes one adaptation is not enough. California sea hares, or sea slugs, live in the mid and low tide zones. To protect themselves from sun and waves they can shrink their soft bodies and hide between rocks.

The sea hare also has other excellent ways to protect itself from **predators**. Its brown, spotted color makes it look like a rock. It is hard for an enemy to find it. If a predator comes too close, the sea hare shoots out purple ink.

Sea urchins are related to sea stars. They belong to the same family. Like sea stars, sea urchins have hundreds of sticky tube feet. Unlike sea stars, sea urchins eat only plants. They have hard teeth to scrape plants from rocks. They also use their hard teeth to grind rocks. They make a hollow in the rocks to use as a home.

Sea urchins are covered in spines. The spines are sharp and contain poison.

The sea star (left) and the sea urchin belong to the same family.

Behavior can also be an adaptation. Many tide pool animals try to fool predators. A crab called the decorator crab covers its shell with seaweed and small shells to keep from being seen!

Mussels are food for sea stars and other tide pool predators. They gather in large groups to stay safe. Periwinkles, oysters, and sand-castle worms also gather together in large groups.

Decorator crabs can disappear among the shells and seaweed in a tide pool.

A sand-castle worm uses its tentacles to catch plankton.

Mussels live next to each other in beds. They do not join their shells together. However, sand-castle worms live together by building one large home. This group home is called a colony. When the tide comes in and covers the colony, the worms use their tentacles to catch food floating in the water.

A Special Glue

Sand-castle worms have a special adaptation that helps them build their tubes. First, the worm collects something like a piece of shell. Then, an organ on its head pushes a blob of glue out onto the shell. The worm wiggles the shell into place and lets the glue set.

Chapter 3

Tide Pool Predators

Tide pools have many predators. There is competition for food. Some tide pool animals have adaptations that help them catch and eat **prey**. Sea stars live on rocks around the tide pool. They move slowly over the rocks on special feet that have sticky suction cups. Their feet stop the sea stars from being washed away.

Sea stars feed on shellfish, such as mussels, that live on the rocks. Sea stars have an amazing way of feeding. They use their sticky feet to open the mussel shells. Then they push their stomachs out through their mouth and into the mussel's shell. They then eat the mussel.

Sea stars can open mussels by pulling them apart with their sticky tube feet.

The octopus is a tide pool predator. It cannot survive out of the water. It swims in the open ocean, but prefers life in the low tide zone. There, it feeds on crabs, snails, and clams.

An octopus has more than one adaptation to help it catch prey. It can change color to look like the rocks or sand around it. It can squeeze its soft body into narrow cracks. The octopus hides and waits, staying alert for small animals passing by. Then it uses its tentacles to grab its prey.

An octopus can hide in a tide pool by changing color to look like sand.

It is good to visit tide pools and learn about the creatures that live there. Some people study tide pools. Some people collect tide pool creatures like sea urchins and mussels for food. Sometimes people and their pets walk through tide pools. Tide pool visitors have to be careful not to harm the creatures that live there.

To help tide pool creatures survive, we should always remember to leave the tide pool as we found it.

The creatures that live in tide pools often have to share their space with humans.

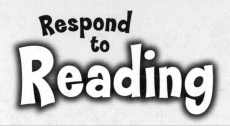

Respond to Reading

Summarize

Use text details from *Life in a Tide Pool* to summarize the selection. Your graphic organizer may help you.

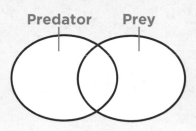

Predator   Prey

Text Evidence

1. How do you know that *Life in a Tide Pool* is expository text? GENRE

2. What do sea stars and sea urchins have in common? What is different?
   COMPARE AND CONTRAST

3. What does the word *scrape* on page 9 mean? What words in the sentence help you understand its meaning? SENTENCE CLUES

4. Write a paragraph comparing an octopus with another tide pool animal. Say what is the same and what is different.
   WRITE ABOUT READING

Compare Texts

Read how the bluebird and the coyote got their colors.

Bluebird and Coyote

Did you know that the first bluebird was brown? Then, one night, the bluebird had a dream.

"Bored with brown?" a voice asked. "It's not too late to change. Just visit the blue lake."

"Is it far?" asked Bluebird.

"Yes, very far," said the voice. "But it's worth it. Bathe in the lake for five mornings and your feathers will turn blue. You will also be very clean."

"Is that all I have to do?" asked Bluebird suspiciously.

"Oh, right, I almost forgot," said the voice. "Sing the 'Ode to Blue' while you bathe."

"How does it go?" asked Bluebird.

"Just make it up," said the voice.

Bluebird did as he was told, and all was well until the fourth morning, when his feathers fell out.

"Can this be right?" he asked, but there was nobody there to hear him. Or so he thought.

To Bluebird's great relief, on the fifth morning, when he came out of the lake, he had beautiful blue feathers.

Meanwhile, a coyote was watching. He had hoped to snack on Bluebird, but seeing those bright blue feathers gave him other ideas.

"How did you do that?" asked Coyote. "You were so drab, but now you look amazing. I want that color!"

Did I mention that Coyote was a dull green?

"Here's what you do," said Bluebird.

Coyote followed the instructions faithfully. His "Ode to Blue" went on for hours. On the fourth day, his fur fell out. And on the fifth day, it grew back, electric blue. "Excellent color!" said Coyote.

Eager to see if his shadow was as beautiful as he was, Coyote whipped his head around. Bang! He ran straight into a tree branch! He fell to the ground and was soon covered in brown dust. Since that day, there has never been a blue coyote, but coyotes still howl a few verses of "Ode to Blue" at the end of the day. Just in case.

Make Connections

In *Bluebird and Coyote,* Coyote turns blue. Would that be a useful adaptation for a coyote?
ESSENTIAL QUESTION

How does being able to change color help some tide pool animals? How does being brown help a coyote? **TEXT TO TEXT**

Glossary

adaptations *(ad-ap-TAY-shuhnz)* changes in animals or plants that fit them better for their environment *(page 6)*

behavior *(bee-HAYV-yuhr)* the way in which something behaves *(page 10)*

habitat *(HAB-ih-tat)* the place where a plant or animal naturally lives or grows *(page 3)*

predators *(PRED-uh-turz)* animals that eat other animals *(page 8)*

prey *(PRAY)* animals that are eaten by other animals *(page 12)*

tentacles *(TEN-tuh-kuhlz)* long, flexible animal parts used for grasping or feeling *(page 2)*

Index

Focus on Science

Purpose To compare and contrast animals by their adaptations.

What to Do

Step 1 ▶ Make a list of six animals that you read about in *Life in a Tide Pool*.

Step 2 ▶ Create a three-column chart with headings like the one below.

Animal	Where They Live	Type of Adaptation

Step 3 ▶ Place each animal from your list in the correct column on the chart.

Step 4 ▶ Brainstorm more animals and add them to the chart.

Conclusion What can you learn by comparing and contrasting animals this way?